THE ULTIMATE
FC BARCELONA
TRIVIA BOOK

A Collection of Amazing Trivia Quizzes
and Fun Facts for Die-Hard Barça Fans!

Ray Walker

Exclusive Free Book
Crazy Sports Stories

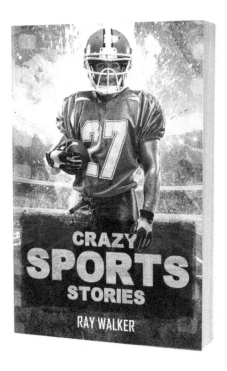

As a thank you for getting a copy of this book I would like to offer you a free copy of my book Crazy Sports Stories which comes packed with interesting stories from your favorite sports such as Football, Hockey, Baseball, Basketball and more.

Grab your free copy over at
RayWalkerMedia.com/Bonus

CONTENTS

INTRODUCTION

FC Barcelona has been a truly fascinating soccer club since being formed back in 1899, and the side is still making history and setting records in 2021. The team is well known for its never-say-die attitude and entertaining style while fielding some of the greatest players to ever grace the game.

Barcelona has set numerous domestic and European records over the years due to their consistent level of excellence, and there's simply no sign of the side slowing down anytime soon.

The outfit is regarded as one of the most successful in sporting history, as well as being one of richest as far as revenue is concerned. Barcelona is really a world-wide phenomenon rather than just a Spanish success story, as the side is followed passionately and loyally by hundreds of millions of fans across the planet.

There have been a few disappointments along the way, of course, since the club has had to settle for runner-up status several times along their journey. However, their trophy room is overflowing with domestic and continental silverware.

With such a strong fan base, Barça should be able to continue with their traditional winning ways season after season, even as star players retire and youngsters are introduced.

This Barcelona trivia and fact book features details on some of the club's greatest players and managers, including Lionel Messi, Johan Cruyff, Pep Guardiola, Andrés Iniesta, Carles Puyol, Xavi, Sergio Busquets, Neymar Jr., Ronaldinho, Luis Suárez, Ronaldo, César Rodríguez, Romário, Antoni Ramallets, Víctor Valdés, and Josep Samitier.

This entertaining book is filled with a tremendous range of facts about the club with 12 different quiz chapters. Each chapter features 20 multiple-choice and true or false questions, with the answers appearing on a later page. Each chapter also adds to the story with 10 historical "Did You Know" facts concerning the club's colorful history.

Barça supporters, refresh your memories with this fact book, re-live the team's history, and perhaps even learn something you weren't aware of along the way. It's the perfect research tool to help prepare yourself for all types of contests and trivia challenges against fellow Barça and soccer fans.

We trust you'll enjoy this journey through time and remind yourself why you've always been such a staunch Barcelona supporter.

CHAPTER 1:

ORIGINS & HISTORY

QUIZ TIME!

1. Which year was FC Barcelona founded in?

    a. 1902

    b. 1899

    c. 1887

    d. 1885

2. The club's original crest was the coat of arms of Barcelona City.

    a. True

    b. False

3. Who was the club's founder?

    a. Otto Kunzle

    b. Bartomeu Terradas

    c. Hans (Joan) Gamper

    d. Walter Wild

4. In which year did the club narrowly avoid bankruptcy?

    a. 1902

    b. 1905

    c. 1908

    d. 1914

5. Which country was Hans (Joan) Gamper originally from?

    a. Switzerland

    b. Netherlands

    c. Denmark

    d. Belgium

6. What is the official shade of red that has graced Barcelona's kits since the club's inception?

    a. Bordeaux

    b. Maroon

    c. Burgundy

    d. Garnet

7. The first version of Barcelona's current crest was adopted in 1910 following a competition to create a new design separate from the city's coat of arms.

    a. True

    b. False

8. How was FC Barcelona founded?

    a. It was an offshoot of a local church team.

    b. Hans (Joan) Gamper printed an ad in the local paper to find like-minded people interested in forming a football club.

c. It was formed after local players won a lottery.

d. The team originated at a Barcelona brewery.

9. Who did Barcelona play their first-ever match against?

    a. FC Català

    b. Team Anglès

    c. Escocès FC

    d. Team Roig

10. What was the outcome of the club's first friendly match?

    a. 0-4 loss

    b. 2-0 win

    c. loss

    d. 7-7 draw

11. What was the first major league Barcelona played in?

    a. Espania Súper Liga

    b. Catalan Regional Liga 2

    c. La Catalan Fútbol Liga

    d. Catalan Football Championship

12. Barcelona originally played at the Hotel Casanovas grounds for the first year of the club's existence.

    a. True

    b. False

13. Which publication did Hans (Joan) Gamper print an advert in to find football players?

    a. *Los Deportes*

    b. *Faro de Vigo*

    c. *La Gazeta*

    d. *La Vanguardia*

14. Who did Barcelona defeat 2-0 in their first-ever La Liga match on February 12, 1929?

    a. Racing de Santander

    b. Atlético Madrid

    c. CE Europa

    d. Real Unión

15. What does Barcelona's slogan, "Més que un club," translate to in English?

    a. A club for everyone

    b. All for the club

    c. Our lone club

    d. More than a club

16. Lluís d'Ossó i Serra scored the club's first goal on December 24, 1899.

    a. True

    b. False

17. What was the club's first official home stadium from 1909 to 1922?

    a. Camp de la Muntaner

    b. Camp de Les Corts

    c. Carretera d'Horta grounds

    d. Camp de la Indústria

18. What color shorts did Barcelona wear for their first 10 years?

    a. Red
    b. White
    c. Black
    d. Green

19. What year did Barcelona move into their current stadium, Camp Nou?

    a. 1957
    b. 1954
    c. 1951
    d. 1949

20. Barcelona began to play professionally in 1899.

    a. True
    b. False

QUIZ ANSWERS

1. B – 1899

2. A – True

3. C – Hans (Joan) Gamper

4. C – 1908

5. A – Switzerland

6. D – Garnet

7. A – True

8. B – Hans (Joan) Gamper printed an ad in the local paper to find like-minded people interested in forming a football club.

9. B – Team Anglès

10. C – 0-1 loss

11. D – Catalan Football Championship

12. B – False

13. A – *Los Deportes*

14. A – Racing de Santander

15. D – More than a club

16. B – False

17. D – Camp de la Indústria

18. B – White

19. A – 1957

20. B – False

DID YOU KNOW?

1. Futbol Club Barcelona of the Spanish top-flight Primera Division of La Liga is commonly known as Barcelona or FCB, with its nicknames being Barça and Blaugrana, with the club's fans being known as Culés, Barcelonistas, Blaugranes, and Azulgranas. The team currently plays its home games at Camp Nou Stadiumin Barcelona, Catalonia, Spain.

2. The origins of FC Barcelona stretch back to 1899 when it was founded by Hans Gamper, also known as Joan Gamper, of Switzerland and a group player from Catalan, Spain, Switzerland, and England. The club's motto is "Més que un club," which means 'more than a club' in English, and the team's official anthem is "Cant del Barça."

3. In October 1899, an advertisement was placed in the *Los Deportes* newspaper by Hans Gamper, who was hoping to form a new football club. In response, 11 players met him at the Gimnasio Solé on November 29, and the club was born. Walter Wild was named the first director, with others in attendance being Lluís d'Ossó i Serra, Bartomeu Terradas, Otto Kunzle, Otto Maier, Enric Ducal, Pere Cabot, Carles Puyol, Josep Llobet, John Parsons, and William Parsons.

4. The new club played its first friendly game on December 8, 1899, against the English colony in Barcelona at the old velodrome in Bonanova. FC Barcelona originally competed in regional and national cup events including the Campionat

de Catalunya and Copa del Rey. The first piece of silverware was hoisted in 1901-02 by winning the Catalan League Championship known as the Copa Macaya. The squad also competed in the inaugural Copa del Rey tournament, losing 2-1 to Bizcaya in the final.

5. In 1908, Hans Gamper was appointed club president to help save it, as the team was struggling both financially and on the pitch. It hadn't won a trophy since the 1905 Campionat de Catalunya. Gamper was determined to save the club and took full responsibility in operating it at that point. In fact, he would act as club president a total of five different times between 1908 and 1925. One of Gamper's main achievements was making sure the team had its own stadium as a way of generating a stable and steady income.

6. On March 14, 1909, the team began playing its home games at a stadium named Camp de la Indústria, which had a capacity for 8,000 fans. In addition, the club held a public contest for a logo design. This was won by Carles Comamala, and his design became the first official club crest. The crest has gone through some minor changes over the years, but in general is quite similar to the original design.

7. Since the club now had a home stadium, Barcelona began to compete in a new competition known as the Pyrenees Cup, which consisted of the some of the nation's top teams and was regarded as the most prestigious tournament of the day. Barcelona was quite successful, as they won the inaugural event in 1910 and the next three as well. The competition

was last held in 1914 and won by Espanyol, but Barcelona won the competition four of the five years it existed.

8. Around the same time as the Pyrenees Cup, FC Barcelona changed its official language to Catalan from Castilian, and became an important part of Catalan identity. By 1922, Gamper had attracted over 20,000 members to the club, and this helped finance a new home ground. The team then moved to its new home, which was known as Les Cortes. The stadium had an original capacity of 30,000, and this was doubled to 60,000 in the 1940s.

9. The club turned professional in 1926, and in 1929 it won the inaugural season of the Spanish League. Unfortunately, just a year later on July 30, 1930, Hans Gamper committed suicide due to depression, which was caused by financial and personal difficulties. The Spanish Civil War then began in 1936, and several Barcelona players fought against the military uprising. During the unrest, club president Josep Sunyol was murdered.

10. Over the years, Barcelona has become one of the strongest soccer teams in the world with a Spanish-record 74 major domestic trophies to its name as of January 2021. The club holds or shares four domestic and three European records for various trophies won, and has won a total of 94 major international and domestic trophies combined.

CHAPTER 2:

THE CAPTAIN CLASS

QUIZ TIME!

1. Who was Barcelona's longest-serving captain as of 2020?

   a. Joan Segarra

   b. Pep Guardiola

   c. José Ramón Alexanko

   d. Carles Puyol

2. Barcelona has named 83 full-time captains in club history.

   a. True

   b. False

3. Who was named captain in 1951?

   a. César Rodrìguez

   b. Joan Segarra

   c. Eduardo Manchón

   d. Gustau Biosca

4. Which player did Barcelona name skipper in 1980?

   a. Carles Rexach

   b. Lobo Carrasco

c. Esteban Vigo

d. Pello Artola

5. Which player was NOT named one of the vice-captains in 2019-20?

    a. Sergi Roberto

    b. Sergio Busquet

    c. Gerard Piqué

    d. Ivan Rakitić

6. How many seasons did Carles Puyol serve as club captain?

    a. 7

    b. 9

    c. 10

    d. 13

7. Barcelona began naming four captains for each season in 2011-12.

    a. True

    b. False

8. Who was named captain in 1986-87?

    a. Ángel Pedraza

    b. Paco Clos

    c. José Ramón Alexanko

    d. Lobo Carrasco

9. Which captain later managed the club?

    a. Johan Cruyff

    b. Carles Puyol

c. Andrés Iniesta

d. Gheorghe Popescu

10. Which player was NOT appointed a vice-captain in the 2010-11 season?

a. Xavier Hernández

b. Víctor Valdés

c. Bojan Krkić

d. Andrés Iniesta

11. What year was Andrés Iniesta appointed skipper?

a. 2015

b. 2013

c. 2017

d. 2014

12. Barcelona named Xavier Hernández captain in his final season with the club.

a. True

b. False

13. How many seasons did José Ramón Alexanko serve as the club's captain?

a. 10

b. 7

c. 4

d. 2

14. Which player captained Barcelona from 1978 to 1980?

a. Ferran Olivella

b. Antoni Torres

c. Johan Cruyff

d. Juan Manuel Asensi

15. Which player was never a full-time club captain?

    a. Pep Guardiola

    b. José Vicente Sánchez

    c. Diego Maradona

    d. Joan Segarra

16. Gheorghe Popescu was Barcelona's first player not born in Spain to be named captain.

    a. True

    b. False

17. Who did Lionel Messi succeed as full-time captain?

    a. Jordi Alba

    b. Sergi Roberto

    c. Andrés Iniesta

    d. Sergio Busquets

18. What year was Tente Sánchez named captain?

    a. 1990

    b. 1985

    c. 1983

    d. 1981

19. Who captained the club from 1997 to 2001?

    a. Pep Guardiola

    b. Luis Enrique

    c. Albert Ferrer

    d. Sergi Barjuán Esclusa

20. Lionel Messi was named captain ahead of the 2018-19 season.

    a. True

    b. False

QUIZ ANSWERS

1. D – Carles Puyol

2. B – False

3. A – César Rodrìguez

4. A – Carles Rexach

5. D – Ivan Rakitić

6. C – 10

7. B – False

8. C – José Ramón Alexanko

9. A – Johan Cruyff

10. C – Bojan Krkić

11. A – 2015

12. A – True

13. B – 7

14. D – Juan Manuel Asensi

15. C – Diego Maradona

16. B – False

17. C – Andrés Iniesta

18. D – 1981

19. A – Pep Guardiola

20. A – True

DID YOU KNOW?

1. There have been approximately 27 full-time captains listed by Barcelona since 1920, with numerous other players acting as vice-captains. As of 2018, Barcelona has used a four-captain system. The players who wear the armband during the season are Lionel Messi, Sergio Busquets, Gerard Piqué, and Sergi Roberto. This system has been used since former skipper Andrés Iniesta left the club. In reality, Messi is the team captain with the other three being vice-captains, when healthy.

2. Midfielder Andrés Iniesta played with the first team between 2002 and 2018 and was a vice-captain with the side before being named skipper in 2015 until leaving in 2018. Iniesta played over 750 matches with the club, making him one of the team's longest-serving players. The Spanish international helped it capture a remarkable 32 major trophies, including nine La Liga titles and four European Champions League crowns. He also received numerous individual honors and is currently the most decorated Spanish footballer ever for club and country.

3. Defender Carles Puyol took over as skipper from Luis Enrique in August 2004 and played his entire career for the club from 1999 to 2014. He wore the armband until retiring, which makes him the longest-serving captain in club history. The former goalkeeper and forward was a Spanish

international who made 663 appearances with the team and helped it win 17 major trophies, including six La Liga and three European Champions League titles.

4. When Carles Puyol hung up his boots in 2014, the captaincy was earned by midfielder Xavier Hernández Creus, who was simply known as Xavi. After graduating from the Barcelona youth system, he played over 500 league contests and a club-record 869 in total with the side from 1998 to 2015 and chipped in with goals. He became the first player in Barça history to play in 150 European and FIFA Club World Cup games combined. He also helped the team hoist 25 major titles, including eight La Liga and four European Champions League titles.

5. Known as "Talin," José Ramón Alexanko wore the captain's armband with pride between 1986 and 1993 and played with the team from 1980 to 1993 after signing from Athletic Bilbao at the age of 24. The Spanish international defender and his teammates excelled under manager Johan Cruyff from the late 1980s to the early 1990s and were typically referred to as "The Dream Team." As skipper, Alexanko led the side to three La Liga titles, a UEFA Cup Winners' Cup, and a European Cup. He would later become an assistant manager with the club between 2000 and 2002.

6. The club's most successful manager, Pep Guardiola, also happened to be one of its best captains too. The Spanish international midfielder was a product of Barcelona's famous La Masia academy and played with the first team

from 1990 to 2001 while wearing the armband between 1997 and 2001. Guardiola helped the club win 14 trophies, including six La Liga titles and a European Cup. When Louis van Gaal took over as manager in the summer of 1997, he quickly gave the armband to Guardiola as a replacement for Gheorghe Popescu.

7. Gheorghe Popescu was a Romanian international defender/midfielder who represented Barça between 1995 and 1997 and captained the side in his last season. He was signed from English Premier League outfit Tottenham Hotspur and joined Galatasary of Turkey when leaving. In between, Popescu helped the team win a Copa del Rey, a Supercopa de España, and a UEFA Cup Winners' Cup. He appeared in just under 100 official games with the club and contributed 13 goals to go along with his leadership skills.

8. One of the team's most successful managers was also one of its greatest players and captains. Dutch international wizard Johan Cruyff suited up with the squad from 1973 to 1978 while serving as captain after his first year. Cruyff, who was recognized as one of the greatest players in the world, had joined from Ajax of Amsterdam for a then world-record transfer fee. He helped his teammates capture a league title and Copa del Rey as a player and won the Ballon d'Or award three times during his career, including 1973 and 1974.

9. For two years in the early 1980s, the team captaincy was entrusted to Spanish international midfielder/defender José

Vicente Sánchez, who was commonly known as "Tente." He started with the club in 1975 as a youth and played with the first team from 1977 to 1986 before leaving for Real Murcia. Sánchez helped lead the squad win 11 trophies as well as a runners-up medal at the 1985-86 European Cup. After hanging up his boots in 1990, Sánchez became a player's agent.

10. Spanish international defender Joan Segarra served as captain between 1961 to 1964 after joining the team in 1949. Segarra helped his team win 15 trophies during his Barça days, including four league titles and six Spanish Cups. After hanging up his boots following 299 league appearances, he later returned to the club as a youth coach manager of the B team and would later be an assistant to first-team manager Helenio Herrera.

CHAPTER 3:

AMAZING MANAGERS

QUIZ TIME!

1. Which manager has won the most major trophies with Barcelona as of 2020?

   a. Louis van Gaal

   b. Luis Enrique

   c. Johan Cruyff

   d. Pep Guardiola

2. Barcelona has had 65 managers as of 2020.

   a. True

   b. False

3. Who was appointed manager in June 2003?

   a. Carles Rexach

   b. Louis van Gaal

   c. Frank Rijkaard

   d. Radomir Antić

4. How many trophies did the club win under Johan Cruyff?

    a. 15
    b. 14
    c. 11
    d. 7

5. Who did Ronald Koeman succeed as manager in August 2020?

    a. Josep Planas
    b. Ernesto Valverde
    c. Gerardo Martino
    d. Quique Setién

6. Which club was Luis Enrique managing before he joined Barcelona?

    a. Celta de Vigo
    b. A.S. Roma
    c. RS Gijón
    d. Barcelona Youth Squad

7. Jack Alderson was the club's first-ever manager in 1899.

    a. True
    b. False

8. Who was appointed manager in May 2017?

    a. Francesc Vilanova
    b. Ernesto Valverde
    c. Quique Setién
    d. Louis Enrique

9. How many major trophies did Pep Guardiola win as manager of Barcelona?

   a. 14

   b. 8

   c. 12

   d. 9

10. Which club did Ronald Koeman manage before coming to Barcelona?

    a. S.L. Benfica

    b. PSV

    c. Everton FC

    d. Southampton FC

11. What year did Pep Guardiola become manager of Barcelona?

    a. 2014

    b. 2006

    c. 2012

    d. 2008

12. Between 2000 and 2010, Barcelona has employed seven different managers.

    a. True

    b. False

13. How many seasons was Frank Rijkaard manager of Barcelona?

    a. 5

    b. 2

c. 7

d. 4

14. How many major trophies did Luis Enrique win in his three years as club manager?

    a. 10

    b. 5

    c. 2

    d. 9

15. Which club did Johan Cruyff manage before joining Barcelona in 1973?

    a. Washington Diplomats

    b. AFC Ajax

    c. Los Angeles Aztecs

    d. Feyenoord

16. Barcelona was the first top-flight team of any league that Pep Guardiola managed.

    a. True

    b. False

17. Which club did Gerardo Martino manage before taking over at Barcelona?

    a. Atlanta United FC

    b. Club Libertad

    c. Newell's Old Boys

    d. Cerro Porteño

18. Who was named manager in May 1996?

    a. Terry Venables
    b. Udo Lattek
    c. Bobby Robson
    d. Llorenç Serra Ferrer

19. Which club was Quique Setién managing before Barça?

    a. CD Lugo
    b. Polideportivo Ejido
    c. UD Las Palmas
    d. Real Betis

20. Carles Rexach was the club's longest-serving manager as of 2020.

    a. True
    b. False

QUIZ ANSWERS

1. D – Pep Guardiola

2. B – False

3. C – Frank Rijkaard

4. C – 11

5. D – Quique Setién

6. A – Celta de Vigo

7. B – False

8. B – Ernesto Valverde

9. A – 14

10. C – Everton FC

11. D – 2008

12. A – True

13. A – 5

14. D – 9

15. B – AFC Ajax

16. A – True

17. C – Newell's Old Boys

18. C – Bobby Robson

19. D – Real Betis

20. B – False

DID YOU KNOW?

1. According to the club's official website, Barcelona has had a total of 63 different acting managers from when the team was formed in 1899 to January 2021, with several of these men having more than one stint with the club. Although he isn't listed as a manager, Hans Gamper, who is regarded as the club's founder, was basically responsible for the side in its formative years and helped the club win 12 combined regional and national cups between 1902 and 1917.

2. When it comes to hoisting silverware, Pep Guardiola has been the club's most successful boss as of January 2021. The former Barça player was in charge of the squad from June 2008 to June 2012 and won a total of 14 trophies. These were: three La Liga and Supercopa de España championships, along with two each of the Copa del Rey, European Champions League, UEFA Super Cup, and FIFA Club World Cup.

3. Tito Vilanova had some big shoes to fill when he took over as manager from Pep Guardiola and held the job from June 2012 to July 2013. The former Barcelona youth player did a fine job as he led the team to the La Liga title in 2012-13. However, Vilanova was suffering health-wise and stepped down from the position. Sadly, he passed away on April 25, 2014, from cancer at the age of 45. He also won the Miguel Muñoz Trophy for his managing performance in 2012-13.

4. Former Barcelona playing legend Johan Cruyff of Holland was the second-most successful official manager with the team, by guiding Barcelona to 11 trophies during his time as head honcho from May 1988 to May 1996. Cruyff hauled in four La Liga titles along with three Supercopa de España, a European Cup, European Super Cup, Copa del Rey, and Cup Winners' Cup.

5. Johan Cruyff was in charge of the team when it was crowned champions of Europe for the first time in 1991-92 in London, England. The team won the trophy in the 37th edition of the European Cup, with the tournament being renamed as the UEFA Champions League the next season in 1992-93. Barcelona's first triumph in the competition coincided with the tournament adopting a group stage for the first time.

6. The first manager to lead the side to a La Liga title was Romà Forns who played with the team between 1903 and 1913. He was then on the board of directors and took over as manager years later, from 1926 to 1929. Forns led the team to the Catalan Football Championship in 1927-28 as well as the Copa del Rey in 1928. Success followed him as Forns's squad won the 1929 La Liga in its inaugural season, when 10 teams competed for the title between the months of February and June.

7. It would be 16 years before Barcelona won another La Liga title, as they didn't achieve the feat again until 1944-45. In charge of the side at that time was Josep Samitier, who ran

the team from June 1944 to July 1947. The Spanish international Samitier played over 350 games with the squad from 1919 to 1932 before jumping ship to join archrivals Real Madrid. He managed Atlético Madrid in 1936, then Nice in France in 1942, before taking over as Barcelona boss. He later worked as a scout for Barça.

8. Enrique Fernández of Uruguay was the first manager to enjoy success in a European tournament when he guided the team to the inaugural Latin Cup championship in 1949. This competition ran from 1949 to 1957 and was also known as Coupe Latine, Coppa Latina, Taça Latina, and Copa Latina. It was a competition for club teams of the Latin European nations of Spain, Portugal, France, and Italy and held at the end of the domestic season. The Latin Cup was generally considered a predecessor of European tournaments such as the European Cup/UEFA Champions League, which began in 1955. Fernández also hoisted a pair of La Liga crowns with Barcelona.

9. The first major European trophy was won by manager Domènec Balmanya, who was another former Barcelona player. He took over in June 1956 and remained on the job until April 1958 and led his side to the Inter-Cities Fairs Cup in 1958. The competition ran from 1955 to 1971 and is seen as the forerunner to the UEFA Cup. The first tournament actually took three seasons to play, from 1955 to 1958, with Barcelona winning it 8-2 on aggregate. Balmanya also won the 1957 Copa del Rey with the team.

10. Two decades passed before Barcelona won another major European title as manager Joaquim Rifé of Spain was at the helm when the team captured the European Cup Winners' Cup in 1978-79. The tournament ran from 1960 to 1969 and was renamed the UEFA Cup Winners' Cup in 1994. Rifé was acting manager from April 1979 to March 1980 and had represented Barcelona over 525 times as a player between 1963 and 1976 while serving as captain for part of his career.

CHAPTER 4:

GOALTENDING GREATS

QUIZ TIME!

1. How many official matches did Víctor Valdés play with Barcelona?

    a. 238
    b. 405
    c. 539
    d. 645

2. Andoni Zubizarreta recorded 15 clean sheets in the 1993-94 La Liga season.

    a. True
    b. False

3. How many matches did Marc-André ter Stegen play in all competitions in 2015-16?

    a. 26
    b. 32
    c. 38
    d. 49

4. Which keeper made 24 La Liga appearances in the 2002-03 season?

    a. Robert Enke

    b. Roberto Bonano

    c. Víctor Valdés

    d. Pepe Reina

5. How many times did Salvador Sadurní win the Ricardo Zamora Trophy?

    a. 0

    b. 5

    c. 1

    d. 3

6. Which keeper played a total of 3,148 minutes in all competitions in 2015-16?

    a. Jasper Cillessen

    b. Marc-André ter Stegen

    c. Jordi Masip

    d. Claudio Bravo

7. Following the club's 1928 Spanish Cup performance, a poem was written about keeper Francisco Platko's play in the tournament.

    a. True

    b. False

8. Which keeper backed up Ruud Hesp for 16 matches in the 1999-2000 La Liga season?

a. Richard Dutruel

b. Francesc Arnau

c. Vítor Baía

d. Carles Busquets

9. How many times did Víctor Valdés win the Ricardo Zamora Trophy?

    a. 5

    b. 2

    c. 7

    d. 4

10. Who played 11 matches as Roberto Bonano's backup in the 2001-02 La Liga season?

    a. Albert Jorquera

    b. Robert Enke

    c. Pepe Reina

    d. Richard Dutruel

11. How many clean sheets did Víctor Valdés keep in all competitions with Barcelona?

    a. 184

    b. 240

    c. 195

    d. 237

12. Javier Urruticoechea became the first Barça keeper to win the IFFHS World's Best Goalkeeper award.

    a. True

    b. False

13. Which keeper won four straight La Liga titles and a European Cup/Champions League with Barcelona?

 a. Pedro María Artola

 b. Andoni Zubizarreta

 c. Salvador Sadurní

 d. Antoni Ramallets

14. How many La Liga appearances did Pepe Reina make for Barcelona?

 a. 20

 b. 49

 c. 11

 d. 30

15. Which keeper played 3,330 minutes in the 1995-96 La Liga season?

 a. Carles Busquets

 b. Jesús Angoy

 c. Francesc Arnau

 d. Julen Lopetegui

16. In the 1994-95 La Liga season, Carles Busquets allowed a total of 41 goals.

 a. True

 b. False

17. How many goals did Andoni Zubizarreta allow in 43 league matches when he won the 1986-87 Ricardo Zamora Trophy?

 a. 33

 b. 25

c. 29

d. 22

18. Which keeper made 37 appearances in the 1996-97 La Liga season?

   a. Ruud Hesp

   b. Julen Lopetegui

   c. Vítor Baía

   d. Jesús Angoy

19. How many games did Víctor Valdés play in all official competitions in 2009-10?

   a. 16

   b. 25

   c. 43

   d. 55

20. Antoni Ramallets was the first keeper for Barcelona to win the Ricardo Zamora Trophy.

   a. True

   b. False

QUIZ ANSWERS

1. C – 539

2. A – True

3. A – 26

4. B – Roberto Bonano

5. D – 3

6. D – Claudio Bravo

7. A – True

8. B – Francesc Arnau

9. A – 5

10. C – Pepe Reina

11. D – 237

12. B – False

13. B – Andoni Zubizarreta

14. D – 30

15. A – Carles Busquets

16. B – False

17. C – 29

18. C – Vítor Baía

19. D – 55

20. B – False

DID YOU KNOW?

1. Spanish and Catalan international keeper and ex-Olympian Ricardo Zamora played with Barcelona from 1919 to 1922 and would later play with Real Madrid. He was nicknamed "El Divino" and was famous for wearing a polo-neck shirt and cloth cap on the pitch. He was well known for his athleticism and courage and is regarded as one of the greatest goalies in history. The Ricardo Zamora Trophy was named in his honor and is presented to the La Liga goalkeeper who posts the best goals-against average during the season. Zamora helped Barça win five trophies while also winning the Zamora award himself three times.

2. Ferenc Plattkó was a Hungarian international who was signed in 1923 to replace the legendary Ricardo Zamora. The inspirational keeper was one of the key members of the club's Golden Age, and he remained with the team until 1930, playing over 200 games and helping the side win nine pieces of silverware. This consisted of six Catalan championships, two Spanish championships, and one league title. Plattkó would later become director of football with the club in 1934-35 and again over 20 years later in 1955-56.

3. Antoni Ramallets played over 500 games with Barça between 1947 and 1961 and earned a well-deserved reputation as being one of the club's best ever at the goalkeeping position. Originally acquired from local club

Europa, the Spanish international was then loaned to Real Valladolid. Known for his agility and reflexes, he was often known as "Gat de Maracaná" (The Maracaná Cat). Ramallets was the backbone of his squads and helped them win a total of 18 trophies, including six league titles and five Spanish Cups. He also won five Ricardo Zamora Trophies.

4. After Antoni Ramallets retired, Barcelona was worried they wouldn't be able to find a worthy successor. However, Spanish international Salvador Sadurní fit the bill perfectly between 1961 and 1976 and quickly earned the trust of his teammates, coaches, and fans. He played 500 games with the side and won three Ricardo Zamora awards and helped his squad capture a league title, three Copa del Rey trophies, and the Inter-Cities Fairs Cup.

5. When manager Johan Cruyff was fielding his famous Dream Team, he relied on Spanish international Andoni Zubizarreta as his number one goalkeeper. As well as being one of the club's best goalies, he was also known for his leadership and motivational abilities both on and off the pitch. Zubizarreta played with the team from 1986 to 1994 and appeared in close to 500 matches. Known as "Zubi," he won the Ricardo Zamora award once and helped the side capture 13 pieces of silverware, including four straight league titles and a European Cup.

6. Víctor Valdés was another Spanish international keeper who combined quality and leadership on the pitch. He may have enjoyed playing behind one of the club's best-ever defensive

units, but Valdés still needed to be on his toes. He starred with the team between 2002 and 2014 and appeared in just over 600 contests, with 442 goals against in 539 official matches. He won the Ricardo Zamora award five times to share the club record with Antoni Ramallets and set a team mark by going 896 minutes without conceding a goal in 2011-12. Valdés is currently the most successful keeper in Barça history, with 26 titles to his name, including six league and three European Champions League crowns.

7. Nicknamed "Urruti," Javier González Urruticoechea tended goal for the team between 1981 and 1988 and won seven titles and a Ricardo Zamora award thanks to his sturdy play. He signed from Espanyol and stood out due to his reflexes, bravery, and leadership qualities. A dramatic penalty-shot save by Urruti away to Valladolid in 1984-85 helped Barça clinch the league. He would also save two penalties in the shootout of the European Cup Final a year later against Steaua Bucuresti, but it wasn't enough to hoist the trophy. Sadly, Urruti passed away in 2001 at the age of 49 following a traffic accident.

8. German international Marc-André ter Stegen joined Barcelona from Borussia Mönchengladbach in 2014 and was still with the club as of January 2021. He's appreciated by the fans and his teammates for his professionalism, as he was patient after arriving and played just seven league games combined during his first two seasons. He's now played over 250 times in all competitions and has graduated to the

number one position. So far, ter Stegen has helped the club win 12 trophies, including four league titles and a European Champions League.

9. One of the best goals-against averages in La Liga history belongs to former Barcelona keeper Claudio Bravo, when he conceded just 19 times in 37 outings for a goals-against average of .51 per game in 2014-15. Bravo, a Chilean international, joined Barça in 2014 from Real Sociedad and played close to 80 times until leaving for Manchester City in 2016. In his first campaign with the club, Bravo helped Barça win a treble of the La Liga, Copa del Rey, and European Champions League and earned the Ricardo Zamora Trophy. Overall, he helped the side capture eight trophies in his two seasons.

10. Another Barcelona keeper who earned a Ricardo Zamora Trophy was Miguel Reina, as he posted a .66 goals-against average in 1972-73 by allowing 21 goals in 34 league outings. Reina played with the side from 1966 to 1973, arriving from Córdoba and departing for Atlético Madrid. In between, he played just four league games in his first three years but would go on to appear in over 100. He helped the side win three trophies and went 824 minutes without conceding a goal at one point in 1972-73, a club record which lasted until November 2011 when it was bettered by Víctor Valdés.

CHAPTER 5:

DARING DEFENDERS

QUIZ TIME!

1. Which defender made 663 appearances in all competitions for Barcelona?

   a. Dani Alves

   b. Carles Puyol

   c. Migueli

   d. Sergi Barjuán

2. In the 1995-96 La Liga campaign, Gheorghe Popescu was shown 11 yellow cards.

   a. True

   b. False

3. How many assists did Frank de Boer earn in all competitions in 2000-01?

   a. 3

   b. 8

   c. 12

   d. 5

4. Which defender scored five goals in the 2014-15 La Liga season?

   a. Jordi Alba
   b. Marc Bartra
   c. Jérémy Mathieu
   d. Gerard Piqué

5. Who tallied 21 assists in all competitions in 2010-11?

   a. Maxwell
   b. Gerard Piqué
   c. Dani Alves
   d. Adriano

6. Who was shown 13 yellow cards in all competitions in 1993-94?

   a. Juan Carlos
   b. Pep Guardiola
   c. Albert Ferrer
   d. Miguel Ángel Nadal

7. Carles Puyol scored 20 career goals in all competitions with Barcelona.

   a. True
   b. False

8. How many yellow cards did Juliano Belletti receive in the 2005-06 La Liga season?

   a. 12
   b. 7

c. 3

d. 9

9. Which player earned six assists in the 2016-17 La Liga season?

    a. Lucas Digne

    b. Sergi Roberto

    c. Samuel Umtiti

    d. Jérémy Mathieu

10. Who was shown 10 yellow cards in all competitions in 1990-91?

    a. Nando

    b. Ricardo Serna

    c. Luis López Rekarte

    d. Sergi

11. Which defender made his league debut in September 1952?

    a. Óscar López

    b. Rafael Márquez

    c. Michael Reiziger

    d. Sigfrid Gracia

12. Ramón Masó was the only defender shown a red card in the 2005-06 La Liga season and received it in his only appearance of the season.

    a. True

    b. False

13. How many goals did Jordi Alba score in the 2019-20 La Liga season?

    a. 10
    b. 2
    c. 6
    d. 14

14. Which defender had a total of six assists in all competitions in 2013-14?

    a. Patric
    b. Sergi Gómez
    c. Martín Montoya
    d. Sergio Busquets

15. Who netted four goals in the 1996-97 La Liga season?

    a. Gheorghe Popescu
    b. Abelardo
    c. Sergi Barjuán
    d. Laurent Blanc

16. Carles Puyol was named to the FIFPro XI team four times.

    a. True
    b. False

17. Which defender joined the club in 2012 from Valencia?

    a. Martín Montoya
    b. Jordi Alba
    c. Sergi Gómez
    d. Marc Bartra

18. Who racked up 17 assists in all competitions in 2018-19?

    a. Nélson Semedo
    b. Sergi Roberto
    c. Clément Lenglet
    d. Jordi Alba

19. In which season did Carles Puyol win the UEFA Club Best Defender award?

    a. 2011-12
    b. 2008-09
    c. 2005-06
    d. 2000-01

20. Rafael Marquez left Barcelona for the New York Red Bulls in 2010.

    a. True
    b. False

QUIZ ANSWERS

1. B – Carles Puyol

2. A – True

3. B – 8

4. D – Gerard Piqué

5. C – Dani Alves

6. C – Albert Ferrer

7. B – False

8. D – 9

9. B – Sergi Roberto

10. A – Nando

11. D – Sigfrid Gracia

12. B – False

13. C – 6

14. C – Martín Montoya

15. A – Gheorghe Popescu

16. B – False

17. B – Jordi Alba

18. D – Jordi Alba

19. C – 2005-06

20. A – True

DID YOU KNOW?

1. One of the club's best left-backs was Spanish international defender Jordi Alba, who stood just 5 feet 7 inches tall. He started out with Valencia and joined Barcelona in 2012. The mobile left-back is technically gifted and doesn't hesitate to join in the attack. As of January 2021, he had helped the team capture five La Liga titles, a European Champions League, four Copa del Reys, three Supercopas de España, and a FIFA Club World Cup. Alba, who has already played over 360 games with Barça, was also named to the La Liga Team of the Season for 2014-15.

2. Spanish international Sigfrid Gracia suited up for Barcelona between 1949 and 1966 and made his La Liga debut in September 1952. He then spent part of his early career on loan with fellow Barcelona-based club España Industrial. He played over 225 league games with Barça and more than 500 in total to help the side capture 11 trophies during his playing days. He finally hung up his boots in the mid-1960s at the age of 34.

3. After beginning his career with Atlas in 1996 in his Mexican homeland, Rafael Marquez found himself in Europe three years later when he joined Monaco. He then arrived in Barcelona in 2003 and played until leaving for the New York Red Bulls in 2010. When in Spain, Marquez helped the squad win a dozen trophies including four La Liga titles and

two European Champions Leagues. Marquez is generally regarded as Mexico's best-ever defender. He played in five straight World Cup tournaments and was capped 147 times for Mexico.

4. Legendary defender Antoni Torres played with Barça between 1965 and 1976 after spending the first two years of his pro career with Hércules de Alicante. He played close to 500 games with Barcelona and helped them hoist the La Liga title in 1973-74, the Copa del Rey in 1967-68 and 1970-71, as well as the Inter-Cities Fairs Cup in 1965-66. Torres played five times for Spain, and after retiring, he managed the Barcelona B team and opened a youth football school in the city.

5. Center-back Migueli Bernardo Bianquetti was nicknamed "Tarzan" and was also known simply as "Migueli." He played over 660 games for the team between 1973 and 1988 after arriving from Cádiz. During the 1978-79 European Cup Winners' Cup, he played with a broken collarbone to help Barça beat Fortuna Düsseldorf 4-3 in extra time. Migueli was named the best Spanish Player in La Liga in 1977-78 and 1984-85 and helped the side win 11 trophies. After hanging up his boots, the Spanish international joined the team's coaching staff and assisted as a sporting advisor.

6. Brazilian international Daniel Alves could also play in the midfield but is generally considered to be one of the top full-backs in the history of the game. He played with the club from 2008 to 2016 after joining from Sevilla and was still

playing in his homeland as of January 2021. Throughout his illustrious career, Alves has helped his teams win 41 trophies, which currently makes him the most decorated player in soccer history. Twenty-six of his trophy wins came with Barça, including six La Liga and three European Champions League titles.

7. Gerard Piqué spent his youth with Barcelona's La Masia football academy but kicked off his pro career in England with Manchester United. He returned to Barça in 2008 and was still with the team as of January 2021. With over 550 appearances and more than 45 goals to his name, Piqué has helped Barça win 29 major trophies, including eight La Liga and three European Champions League crowns. His average passes-completed ratio with the team has typically been in the 90% range throughout his career, and he's also a been key player for the national side with over 100 caps earned.

8. As recently as January 2021, former Dutch international defender Ronald Koeman was still managing Barcelona after being appointed in August 2020. Known for his accurate and powerful long-range shots and free kicks, Koeman netted 106 goals in 350 appearances with the team with one of his most important free kick markers helping Barça capture the 1992 European Cup. Koeman played on the Dream Team under manager Johan Cruyff and won four straight La Liga titles between 1991 and 1994. The top-scoring defender in Barcelona annals helped the side win 12 trophies in total.

9. Between 1993 and 2002, Sergi Barjuán, known simply as

"Sergi" by most, was basically a fixture at left-back with Barcelona. He graduated through the club's youth ranks and made his first-team debut in a European Champions League match. Sergi formed an effective partnership with right-back Albert "Chapi" Ferrer and wore the captain's armband in 2001-02 when Pep Guardiola left. Sergi appeared in 460 games with the team and helped it win 10 pieces of silverware, including three La Liga titles and a European Cup Winners' Cup.

10. Joaquim Rifé played 562 games with Barça from 1964 to 1976 and spent 1971 to 1973 as captain while going on to manage the side between 1979 and 1980. He started his career as a winger, then moved to the midfield and finally to the back four, but always hung on to his attacking instincts as he scored 61 goals for the squad. He also played four times for the Spanish national team with a goal to his name. Rifé returned to Barça as the technical director of youth football from 2000 to 2003. As a player, he helped the side capture the La Liga in 1973-74, the Copa del Rey in 1967-68 and 1970-71, and the Inter-Cities Fairs Cup in 1965-66.

CHAPTER 6:

MAESTROS OF THE MIDFIELD

QUIZ TIME!

1. How many assists did Xavi Hernández post in the 2003-04 La Liga season?

   a. 15
   b. 7
   c. 12
   d. 4

2. Michael Laudrup left Barcelona for Real Madrid in 1994.

   a. True
   b. False

3. Which player made 567 appearances with the club?

   a. Pep Guardiola
   b. Guillermo Amor
   c. Luis Enrique
   d. Javier Mascherano

4. Who scored eight goals in all competitions in 2016-17?

    a. Rafinha
    b. Ivan Rakitić
    c. André Gomes
    d. Javier Mascherano

5. Which midfielder played 3,255 minutes in the 2019-20 La Liga season?

    a. Arthur
    b. Ivan Rakitić
    c. Arturo Vidal
    d. Frenkie de Jong

6. How many goals did Luis Enrique score in the 1998-99 La Liga season?

    a. 18
    b. 14
    c. 11
    d. 6

7. Andrés Iniesta won the FIFA World Player of the Year in 2012.

    a. True
    b. False

8. Who earned 21 assists in all competitions in 2009-10?

    a. Jonathan dos Santos
    b. Víctor Sánchez
    c. Xavi Hernández
    d. Yaya Touré

9. How many assists did Andrés Iniesta record in the 2008-09 La Liga season?

    a. 8
    b. 11
    c. 14
    d. 16

10. Which midfielder tallied 12 goals in the 1998-99 La Liga season?

    a. Luis Enrique
    b. Phillip Cocu
    c. Roger García
    d. Albert Celades

11. Which midfielder was once a full-time Barça captain?

    a. Riqui Puig
    b. Arthur
    c. Carles Aleñá
    d. José Mari Bakero

12. Cesc Fàbregas posted 10 assists in the 2011-12 La Liga season.

    a. True
    b. False

13. Which player was shown 11 yellow cards in all competitions in 2001-02?

    a. Fábio Rochemback
    b. Gerard López

c. Roberto Trashorras

d. Xavi Hernández

14. How many total games did Diego Maradona play with Barcelona?

   a. 52

   b. 75

   c. 103

   d. 265

15. How many goals did Johan Neeskens score with Barça in his 233 contests?

   a. 39

   b. 44

   c. 54

   d. 85

16. Rafinha scored six goals in the 2015-16 La Liga season.

   a. True

   b. False

17. How many goals did Cesc Fàbregas notch in all competitions in 2011-12?

   a. 25

   b. 8

   c. 20

   d. 15

18. Which midfielder was shown nine yellow cards in all competitions in 2009-10?

a. Thiago Alcântara

b. Víctor Sánchez

c. Yaya Touré

d. Seydou Keita

19. How many times did Andrés Iniesta make the FIFPro XI team as a member of Barcelona?

a. 12

b. 9

c. 6

d. 3

20. Yaya Touré played a total of 174 La Liga games for Barcelona.

a. True

b. False

QUIZ ANSWERS

1. C – 12

2. A – True

3. B – Guillermo Amor

4. B – Ivan Rakitić

5. D – Frenkie de Jong

6. C – 11

7. B – False

8. C – Xavi Hernández

9. C – 14

10. B – Phillip Cocu

11. D – José Mari Bakero

12. A – True

13. A – Fábio Rochemback

14. B – 75

15. C – 54

16. B – False

17. D – 15

18. D – Seydou Keita

19. B – 9

20. B – False

DID YOU KNOW?

1. Creative Danish international Micheal Laudrup was a member of Barcelona's Dream Team under manager Johan Cruyff and played in almost every match between 1989 and 1994. He joined the club from Juventus and tallied 97 goals in 296 appearances for the La Liga side during his stay while helping it win 11 titles, including four straight league honors and the 1991-92 European Cup. Laudrup was left out of the starting lineup for the 1993-94 European Cup Final though, after a fallout with Cruyff, and Barcelona was hammered 4-0 by AC Milan. Laudrup then left for Real Madrid soon after.

2. Johan Neeskens was a Dutch international who was nicknamed "Johan Segon" (Johan the Second) and played with the club from 1974 to 1979, meaning he spent a few years on the pitch with fellow countryman Johan Cruyff. A tireless worker, Neeskens helped the side win a Copa del Rey in 1977-78 and a UEFA Cup Winners' Cup in 1978-79. He also chipped in with 54 goals in 233 outings before leaving to join the New York Cosmos. Neeskens was named the La Liga Foreign Player of the Year for 1975-76 and later returned to Barcelona to assist manager Frank Rikjaard.

3. Defensive midfielder Sergio Busquets joined the club in 2005 as a youth and, as of January 2021, was still with the team and had made over 600 appearances. He had played 120 times with the Spanish national team by then as well.

Busquets's father Carles also played with Barça as a backup goalkeeper between 1990 and 1999 after joining the youth academy 22 years before his son. Sergio Busquets has acted as a vice-captain with the team and has helped it win 29 titles, including eight La Liga honors and three European Champions Leagues. He was also named to the La Liga Team of the Season for 2015-16.

4. One of Barcelona's most consistent and creative foreign-born midfielders was Brazilian-born, Portuguese international Anderson Luis de Souza, known as "Deco." The brilliant tactician joined the team from Porto in 2004, where he had already won a European Champions League, and stayed until 2008 when he joined Chelsea. Deco was brought to Barça due to his team spirit and will to win and helped the side capture two straight La Liga titles and the European Champions League, along with four other honors. Deco was a complete player who combined hard work with his technical skill and netted 28 goals in 188 outings with the squad.

5. Guillermo Amor was a Spanish international midfielder who appeared in a Barcelona shirt 567 times and contributed 92 goals. He grew up in the club's youth system and played regularly with the first team from 1988 to 1998. In March 1996, the solid performer was credited with scoring Barcelona's 4,000[th] La Liga goal. With 17 trophies under his belt, Amor had collected the most pieces of major silverware at the club when he left in 1998 to join Fiorentina in Italy. He

then returned to Barcelona as head of youth football between 2003 and 2007, then later became technical director of football training before taking charge of professional youth football with the club.

6. Former captain José Mari Bakero spent 1988 to 1996 with Barça, and the tireless attacking midfielder with great heading abilities was one of the engines which drove the Dream Team. He tallied 115 goals in 432 matches with the side, with his 1991-92 European Cup marker in the knockout stage being one of the most memorable. Trailing 3-0 away to Kaiserslautern in the second leg, Bakero scored with just 30 seconds remaining to save the tie. Barcelona then went on to win their first European Cup a few months later. The Spanish international won 14 trophies with the team and, in 2017, joined Guillermo Amor in taking charge of professional youth football at the club.

7. Known as one of the world's greatest footballers, Diego Maradona spent 1982 to 1984 with Barcelona after leaving Boca Juniors in his homeland of Argentina. Known as "Pelusa," Maradona suffered from injury and hepatitis during his stint with Barça but still managed to drill home 45 goals in 75 matches and helped the side win the Copa del Rey and League Cup in 1982-83 and the Spanish Super Cup in 1983-84. After relations between Maradona and the Barcelona board deteriorated, he left to join Italian side Napoli.

8. German international Bernd Schuster was one of the team's driving forces from 1980 to 1988 and registered 118 goals in

300 outings. Known as "der Blonde Enge" (The Blonde Angel), he was a pillar of strength in the midfield and also possessed exceptional dribbling skills. He often played alongside Diego Maradona from 1982 to 1984 and helped his team win the league in 1984-85, as well as seven other pieces of silverware. Like Maradona, Shuster's relationship with management began to sour, and he didn't play a game in 1986-87. He returned to the side the next season and then left for Real Madrid.

9. After spending his youth career with Barça from 1958 to 1960 and then two years on loan with Osasuna, Josep Maria Fusté became a great on-field leader with the first team from 1962 to 1972. Due to his speed, Fusté was known as "la llebre de Linyola" (The Linyola Hare). The explosive Spanish international possessed tremendous ball skills and could shoot just as well with either foot. He netted 117 goals in 406 encounters and helped the team win three Copa del Rey titles and an Inter-Cities Fairs Cup. After retiring, Fusté became head of the ex-players organization and then a consultant to the club's board.

10. One of the finest technical midfielders at Barcelona was Jesús Maria Pereda, who was nicknamed "Chus" by the fans but known as "Gunpowder" to his teammates due to his on-pitch temperament. He also had a knack for scoring goals, as he notched 111 of them in 317 matches. He joined the team in 1961 from Sevilla and remained for eight seasons during a lean spell, helping the side win the Copa del Rey in 1962-63

and the Inter-Cities Fairs Cup in 1965-66. The Spanish international left the side in 1969 and hung up his boots three years later to enter football management.

CHAPTER 7:

SENSATIONAL STRIKERS & FORWARDS

QUIZ TIME!

1. Which player scored 30 goals in the 1993-94 La Liga season?

    a. Romário

    b. Hristo Stoichkov

    c. Txiki Begiristain

    d. José Mari Bakero

2. Zlatan Ibrahimović joined Barça from Inter Milan in 2009.

    a. True

    b. False

3. Luis Suárez scored how many goals in total with Barcelona during his career from 2014 to 2020?

    a. 160

    b. 177

    c. 210

    d. 304

4. Which player scored nine goals in the 2019-20 La Liga season?

    a. Martin Braithwaite

    b. Ousmane Dembélé

    c. Ansu Fati

    d. Antoine Griezmann

5. How many goals did Ronaldinho score in all competitions in 2006-07?

    a. 15

    b. 19

    c. 24

    d. 30

6. Which player tallied 11 goals in all competitions in 2013-14?

    a. Sandro Ramírez

    b. Pedro

    c. Adama Traoré

    d. Paco Alcácer

7. Winger Hristo Stoichkov was shown two red cards in the 1991-92 La Liga campaign.

    a. True

    b. False

8. How many goals did Neymar Jr. score in the 2013-14 La Liga season?

    a. 15

    b. 12

c. 9

d. 6

9. Who tallied 15 goals in the 1992-93 La Liga season?

    a. José Mari Bakero

    b. Julio Salinas

    c. Txiki Begiristain

    d. Michael Laudrup

10. Which player scored 19 goals in the 2018-19 La Liga season?

    a. Carles Aleñá

    b. Ousmane Dembélé

    c. Philippe Coutinho

    d. Luis Suárez

11. How many La Liga matches did Ronaldo play with Barcelona in 1996-97?

    a. 19

    b. 24

    c. 29

    d. 37

12. Patrick Kluivert was once called "the perfect striker" by manager Louis van Gaal.

    a. True

    b. False

13. How many times did Johan Cruyff win the Ballon d'Or?

    a. 0

    b. 3

c. 4

d. 5

14. Which player tallied 16 assists in all competitions in 2001-02?

    a. Patrick Kluivert

    b. Javier Saviola

    c. Marc Overmars

    d. Rivaldo

15. How many goals did Michael Laudrup score in the 1991-92 La Liga season?

    a. 21

    b. 18

    c. 15

    d. 11

16. In 1994, Romário became the first Barcelona player to win the FIFA World Player of the Year award.

    a. True

    b. False

17. Lionel Messi recorded how many assists in the 2019-20 La Liga season?

    a. 10

    b. 15

    c. 19

    d. 22

18. Which player earned 17 assists in all competitions in 2006-07?

a. Ronaldinho

b. Deco

c. Samuel Eto'o

d. Eidur Gudjohnsen

19. How many times has Lionel Messi been named to the FIFPro XI squad as of 2020?

a. 16

b. 14

c. 11

d. 8

20. In 1960, Luis Suárez Miramontes became the first Barcelona player to win the Ballon d'Or award.

a. True

b. False

QUIZ ANSWERS

1. A – Romário

2. A – True

3. C – 210

4. D – Antoine Griezmann

5. C – 24

6. B – Pedro

7. A – True

8. C – 9

9. C – Txiki Begiristain

10. D – Luis Suárez

11. D – 37

12. A – True

13. B – 3

14. A – Patrick Kluivert

15. C – 15

16. A – True

17. D – 22

18. B – Deco

19. B – 14

20. A – True

DID YOU KNOW?

1. Playing in the midfield and on the wing for Barcelona, Ronaldo de Assis Moreira, more commonly known as "Ronaldinho," joined the team in 2003 from Paris Saint-Germain and remained until 2008 when he joined AC Milan. The pony-tailed Brazilian international won eight trophies with the side, including two La Liga titles and a European Champions League. While with the club, he was named FIFA World Player of the Year twice, the La Liga Best Foreign Player twice, was named to the UEFA Team of the Year three times and won the Ballon d'Or. Ronaldinho notched 110 goals in 250 appearances with the team and set up dozens more with his exquisite playmaking skills.

2. Brazilian international Neymar rocked the La Liga with Barcelona from 2013 to 2017 after arriving from Santos FC in his homeland. He quickly became one of squad's most important players even though he was just 21 years old at the time. It took him a little while to score his first league goal, but they started to flow freely after that, playing up front with Lionel Messi and Luis Suárez. Neymar appeared in just under 200 official games with the club and notched 105 goals before being sold to Paris Saint-Germain for a world-record €222 million in 2017. While in Barcelona, he helped the club capture eight trophies, including a European Champions League, Copa del Rey, and La Liga treble in 2014-15.

3. Swedish international Zlatan Ibrahimović has been a scoring machine at every club he's played with, including Barcelona from 2009 to 2010. He joined from Inter Milan for a reported €66 million fee while striker Samuel Eto'o left Barça for Inter Milan in the somewhat complicated deal. Ibrahimović scored 22 goals in 46 outings before suddenly being loaned to AC Milan in the summer of 2010, with the Italian club eventually buying the player. The controversial Ibrahimović stated that he didn't get along with Barça manager Pep Guardiola and left town after helping the side win the La Liga, two Supercopa de España crowns, the UEFA Super Cup, and the FIFA Club World Cup.

4. Thierry Henry was another of his era's top scorers and played with Barcelona from 2007 and 2010. He joined from Arsenal in England for a reported €24 million and would leave for the New York Red Bulls. In his first season with Barça, Henry led the team with 19 goals while playing on the wing and followed up with 26 the next campaign. He tallied 49 goals in 121 matches, for a goals-per-game ratio of .45, before leaving for America. He helped the squad hoist seven trophies, including a La Liga, Copa del Rey, and European Champions League treble in 2008-09.

5. With 24 goals in his first 75 appearances with Barcelona, Antoine Griezmann may very well end up being worth the controversial €120 million buyout clause the club paid Atlético Madrid for him in 2019. The French international has scored over 200 goals in his club career, which also

includes a stint with Real Sociedad from 2009 to 2014, and he's notched 33 goals in his first 86 contests for his country. Griezmann has yet to help Barcelona win a trophy as of January 2021, but at the age of 29, he should be reaching the peak of his career.

6. Alexis Sánchez could play any forward position and notched 47 goals in 141 games for the club between 2011 and 2014, equating to a goal every three games on average. He joined from Italian side Udinese in July 2011 for a reported €26 million and became the first Chilean to suit up with Barça. Sánchez helped the club win a La Liga, Copa del Rey, UEFA Super Cup, Spanish Super Cup, and FIFA Club World Cup championship during his stint, but his 2012-13 campaign was hampered by several injuries. He then left for Arsenal in England in the summer of 2014.

7. Before Cristiano Ronaldo came along, the "Ronaldo" name had already been made famous by Brazilian international Ronaldo Luiz Nazario. He joined Barcelona from from PSV Eindhoven of Holland in 1996 as a promising young striker and lived up to the hype. Ronaldo played just one season but drilled home 47 goals in 51 appearances. He possessed speed and delicate skills for a big man and helped Barça win a UEFA Cup Winners' Cup, the Copa del Rey, and the Spanish Super Cup. Although he was just 20 years old at the time, Ronaldo, his agents, and the club's board of directors didn't always see eye to eye, and he soon departed for Inter Milan in 1997.

8. Another Brazilian international to leave his mark at Barcelona in such a short time after arriving from PSV Eindhoven was Romário de Souza, better known as "Romário." He joined the squad in 1993 and tallied a league-high 30 goals in 33 league games thanks to his dribbling skills, pace, and shooting accuracy. Barça won the league title and Spanish Super Cup that season, and Romário helped Brazil win the 1994 World Cup while being named Player of the Tournament. He was also named FIFA World Player of the Year for 1994. However, he developed a rift with manager Johan Cruyff and left the team for Flamengo of Brazil after scoring 53 times in 84 contests for Barça.

9. Spanish international striker Enrique Castro González was more commonly known as "Quini" and joined Barcelona in 1980 from Sporting Gijón where he had already won three Golden Boot Awards. Quini was kidnapped at gunpoint in March 1981 but was rescued unharmed by the police 25 days later. With Barça, he won two more Golden Boots in 1980-81 and 1981-82 and netted the team's 3,000th La Liga goal in January 1982. Quini returned to Sporting in 1984 after scoring 101 goals in 181 matches with Barcelona and helping them win five trophies.

10. Gary Lineker will go down in history as one of England's greatest scorers, as he netted 48 goals in 80 games for his country and amassed close to 300 more in his club career. Lineker was one of the few English players to suit up for Barcelona. He joined from Everton in 1986 and stayed until

1989 when he returned to England to play for Tottenham Hotspur. He scored 42 times in 103 league matches and 52 times overall for the team including twice on his debut. Lineker helped the side win the Copa del Rey in 1987-88 and the European Cup Winners' Cup the following season. He was also runner-up for the 1986 Ballon d'Or award.

CHAPTER 8:

NOTABLE TRANSFERS & SIGNINGS

QUIZ TIME!

1. Which player was Barcelona's costliest signing as of 2020, worth a reported transfer fee of €145 million?

    a. Philippe Coutinho

    b. Ousmane Dembélé

    c. Antoine Griezmann

    d. Neymar Jr.

2. Ronaldo was was sold for a record transfer fee of €122 million.

    a. True

    b. False

3. Which club did Barcelona acquire Ronaldinho from in 2003-04?

    a. Paris Saint-Germain

    b. Juventus

c. Liverpool FC

d. Sevilla FC

4. When Barcelona acquired Neymar Jr. in 2013-14, what was the reported transfer fee they paid?

   a. €92.4 million

   b. €90 million

   c. €88.2 million

   d. €64.5 million

5. Which player did Barcelona sign for a reported €24 million in 2007-08?

   a. Yaya Touré

   b. Éric Abidal

   c. Gabriel Milito

   d. Thierry Henry

6. Which player did the club sell to Real Madrid for a reported transfer fee of €60 million in 2000-01?

   a. Mikel Arteta

   b. Luís Figo

   c. Ronald de Boer

   d. Frédéric Déhu

7. In 2009, Barcelona signed Zlatan Ibrahimović for a reported fee of €66 million with Samuel Eto'o joining Inter Milan in the transaction.

   a. True

   b. False

8. Which club was Dani Alves playing for before he joined Barcelona in 2008-09?

   a. Sevilla FC
   b. EC Bahia
   c. Desportivo Brasil
   d. Celta de Vigo

9. Barcelona signed Johan Cruyff for a world-record transfer fee of approximately how much in 1973-74?

   a. €1.3 million
   b. €2 million
   c. €4.8 million
   d. €5.25 million

10. Barcelona signed Rivaldo from which club in 1997-98?

   a. Santa Cruz FC
   b. Mogi Mirim EC
   c. Deportivo La Coruña
   d. SE Palmeiras

11. Which club did Barcelona transfer Ronaldo to in 1997?

   a. Inter Milan
   b. PSV Eindhoven
   c. Real Madrid
   d. AC Milan

12. Barcelona sold Neymar Jr. to Paris Saint-Germain in 2017 for a record transfer fee of €222 million.

   a. True
   b. False

13. What was the transfer fee Barcelona reportedly paid Arsenal FC to acquire Marc Overmars in 2000-01?

    a. €6 million
    b. €12.95 million
    c. €26 million
    d. €40 million

14. Who was Barcelona's most expensive signing in 2019-20?

    a. Frenkie de Jong
    b. Malcom
    c. Miralem Pjanić
    d. Antoine Griezmann

15. What was the reported transfer fee Barcelona paid to acquire Samuel Eto'o from RCD Mallorca in 2004-05?

    a. €32.25 million
    b. €27 million
    c. €16.85 million
    d. €12 million

16. In 2014-15, Barcelona signed five players for €15 million or more each.

    a. True
    b. False

17. Which club did Barcelona sign Luis Suárez from in 2014-15?

    a. FC Groningen
    b. Arsenal FC
    c. AFC Ajax
    d. Liverpool FC

18. What was the transfer fee that Barcelona reportedly paid to sign Cesc Fàbregas in 2011-12?

    a. €14 million
    b. €22.8 million
    c. €34 million
    d. €45.65 million

19. Who was the club's most expensive signing in 2016-17 at a reported €37 million?

    a. Samuel Umtiti
    b. André Gomes
    c. Paco Alcácer
    d. Arda Turan

20. Barcelona paid a transfer fee of just €55 million to acquire Luis Suárez in 2014.

    a. True
    b. False

QUIZ ANSWERS

1. A – Philippe Coutinho

2. B – False

3. A – Paris Saint-Germain

4. C – €88.2 million

5. D – Thierry Henry

6. B – Luís Figo

7. A – True

8. A – Sevilla FC

9. B – €2 million

10. C – Deportivo La Coruña

11. A – Inter Milan

12. A – True

13. D – €40 million

14. D – Antoine Griezmann

15. B – €27 million

16. B – False

17. D – Liverpool FC

18. C – €34 million

19. B – André Gomes

20. B – False

DID YOU KNOW?

1. The top five transfer fees reportedly paid by Barcelona in club history are as follows: Midfielder Philippe Coutinho from Liverpool in 2017-18 for €145 million; Winger Ousmane Dembélé from Borussia Dortmund in 2017-18 for €130 million; Forward Antoine Griezmann from Atlético Madrid in 2019-20 for €120 million; Winger Neymar from Santos FC in 2013-14 for €88.2 million; and Midfielder Frenkie de Jong from Ajax Amsterdam in 2019-20 for €86 million.

2. The top five transfer fees reportedly received by Barcelona for players sold are as follows: Winger Neymar to Paris Saint-Germain in 2017-18 for €222 million; Midfielder Arthur to Juventus FC in 2020-21 for €72 million; Winger Luís Figo to Real Madrid in 2000-01 for €60 million; Forward Alexis Sánchez to Arsenal FC in 2014-15 for €42.5 million; and Midfielder Paulinho to Guangzhou Evergrande Taobao in China for €42 million.

3. Brazilian international Philippe Coutinho spent time with Inter Milan, Vasco da Gama, and Espanyol before Liverpool bought him for a reported €13 million. After 54 goals in 201 appearances, Liverpool sold him to Barcelona in January 2018 for a club-record €145 million. Coutinho notched 21 goals in his first 76 appearances with Barça before being loaned to Bayern Munich for the 2019 campaign, where he scored 11 goals in 38 games. He then returned to Barcelona

in 2020-21 under new manager Ronald Koeman and netted three goals in his first 14 outings. Since joining Barcelona, he's helped the squad win the La Liga title in 2017-18 and 2018-19, along with the Copa del Rey in 2017-18 and the Supercopa de España in 2018.

4. Portuguese international attacker Luís Figo was one of the greatest players of his generation and joined Barcelona from Sporting Lisbon in 1995 for a reported €3 million. He helped the club win five trophies while scoring 45 times in 249 contests. In July 2000, Figo joined Real Madrid as Barça's rivals met the buyout clause in his contract. Barcelona supporters felt betrayed and let him know it when Figo returned to Barcelona for a game in October 2000. Banners hung around the stadium that read "Judas," "Traitor," and "Mercenary," and Figo was taunted mercilessly throughout the contest by verbal abuse and a barrage of objects thrown his way.

5. Turkish midfielder Arda Turan was bought from Atlético Madrid in the summer of 2015 for approximately €34 million after playing there for four seasons and helping the team win the 2013-14 La Liga title and reach the European Champions League Final. He started just 23 La Liga games over the next two seasons and was loaned to Istanbul Basaksehir in 2017-18. He received a 10-game ban for pushing an assistant referee while on loan and was later handed a 32-month suspended jail sentence for a 2018 altercation in an Istanbul nightclub and later firing a gun

into the ground at a local hospital. Turan never played another game for Barça.

6. Jérémy Mathieu was a French defender who joined Barcelona for a reported €20 million in 2014 from fellow La Liga side Valencia. He was expected to help fill the void left by the departed Carles Puyol and Eric Abidal but struggled to do so. Mathieu spent three seasons with Barça, and even though he helped the team win nine trophies, he played just 62 league games and was allowed to leave on a free transfer for Sporting Lisbon in the summer of 2017.

7. After five solid seasons with Arsenal of the English Premier League, Belgian international defender Thomas Vermaelen was bought from the London club for approximately €18 million in August 2014. However, his time with Barça was a bit of a nightmare due to constant injuries. Vermaelen played just one league game in his first campaign, which came about nine months after originally signing. He was loaned to Roma in Italy for the 2016-17 season and would play just 53 times with Barcelona before leaving for Vissel Kobe of Japan in July 2019.

8. Malcom Filipe Silva de Oliveira was simply known as Malcolm by football fans, and they witnessed Barcelona pay approximately €41 million to Bordeaux of France for the forward's services in July 2018. It didn't come easy, though, as Italian side Roma believed they had a deal in place for the player and fans were reportedly waiting at the Rome airport to greet the club's new signing. When Malcom didn't show

up, Roma wasn't too happy and threatened legal action against Barça. Malcolm wasn't really needed at Barcelona, however, and after just 15 league appearances, he was sold to Zenit Saint Petersburg of Russia the next summer.

9. Argentine international defender/midfielder Javier Mascherano was bought from Liverpool in August 2010 for a reported €24 million. He remained for almost eight years before leaving for Hebei China Fortune in January 2018. With Barça, Mascherano appeared in over 300 games and scored just a solitary goal. However, he was a key player as he helped the squad haul in 19 trophies, including five La Liga and two European Champions League titles. He was also named the team Player of the Season for 2013-14.

10. Bayern Munich sold Chilean international midfielder Arturo Vidal to Barcelona in August 2018 for a reported €18 million. He would score 11 goals in 96 games with the club while helping them win the 2018-19 La Liga and Supercopa de España in 2018. However, in September 2020, Vidal was suddenly gone as he was sent to Inter Milan on what was reported a free transfer with a fee of €1 million in variables included. With the Covid-19 pandemic hitting the world in 2020 and reports of Barcelona's debts skyrocketing, some fans believe the 2016 Chilean Footballer of the Year was transferred simply as a way to reduce the squad's salary.

CHAPTER 9:

ODDS & ENDS

QUIZ TIME!

1. How many matches did Barcelona win in their debut La Liga season?

    a. 16
    b. 11
    c. 9
    d. 3

2. Barcelona has been relegated two times as of 2020.

    a. True
    b. False

3. Which team makes up the other half of Barcelona's famous "El Clásico" rivalry?

    a. Athletic Bilbao
    b. Valencia CF
    c. Atlético Madrid
    d. Real Madrid

4. How old was Lionel Messi when he first signed forms with Barcelona?

   a. 17
   b. 15
   c. 13
   d. 10

5. Which local club does Barcelona have a deep-rooted rivalry with that is referred to as the "Derbi Barceloni"?

   a. CE Europa
   b. RCD Espanyol
   c. CE Júpiter
   d. UE Cornellà

6. How many goals did Barcelona score in their first La Liga season?

   a. 46
   b. 37
   c. 34
   d. 23

7. The nickname of Barcelona's supporters, "culers," translates in English to "people who show their backsides."

   a. True
   b. False

8. Who was the youngest first-team player ever for Barcelona, making his debut at the age of 15?

   a. Ansu Fati
   b. Lionel Messi

c. Bojan Krkić

d. Paulino Alcántara

9. In 2016-17, the club set a record for the most goals scored in a 38-game La Liga season with how many?

a. 93

b. 99

c. 116

d. 122

10. Which club did Barcelona defeat 18-0 in the Copa Macaya tournament of 1900-01 for the club's largest margin of victory in any competition?

a. FC Internacional

b. Català FC

c. AUF Tarragona

d. Club Franco-Español

11. Which club did Barcelona defeat 8-0 in a 2014-15 La Liga away match?

a. Málaga CF

b. Celta de Vigo

c. SD Eibar

d. Córdoba CF

12. As of 2020, six different players for Barcelona have won the Ballon d'Or.

a. True

b. False

13. What is the most points Barcelona has recorded in a La Liga season?

    a. 87
    b. 94
    c. 100
    d. 104

14. What does Barcelona's nickname, "blaugrana," translate to in English?

    a. Red stripes
    b. Blue and red
    c. Royal blues
    d. Blue stripes

15. How many different Barcelona players have been named to the FIFPro XI as of 2020?

    a. 5
    b. 7
    c. 10
    d. 14

16. As manager, Johan Cruyff innovated the sport by introducing the style of play known as "tiki-taka."

    a. True
    b. False

17. Who was the oldest player to make an appearance for Barcelona at the age of 38 years old?

    a. José Manuel Pinto
    b. Antoni Ramallets

c. José Ramón Alexanko

d. Joan Segarra

18. In 2010-11, Barcelona went on a La Liga winning streak of how many games?

a. 20

b. 16

c. 12

d. 9

19. What was the most wins Barcelona has posted in a La Liga season as of 2020?

a. 25

b. 28

c. 32

d. 35

20. Lionel Messi's first contract was signed for the club by Carles Rexach on a napkin.

a. True

b. False

QUIZ ANSWERS

1. B – 11

2. B – False

3. D – Real Madrid

4. C – 13

5. B – RCD Espanyol

6. B – 37

7. A – True

8. D – Paulino Alcántara

9. C – 116

10. C – AUF Tarragona

11. D – Córdoba CF

12. A – True

13. C – 100

14. B – Blue and red

15. D – 14

16. A – True

17. A – José Manuel Pinto

18. B – 16

19. C – 32

20. A – True

DID YOU KNOW?

1. Barcelona is owned and operated by the club's supporters rather than a private entity, which means memberships can be purchased but not shares. It's regarded as one of the richest sports organizations in the world and is typically the richest soccer club on the globe on a yearly basis when it comes to revenue. In November 2018, it was reported that Barcelona was the highest-paid sports squad on the planet with the average first-team player being paid just over £10 million ($13.8 million) a year.

2. The FC Barcelona club also includes several other sporting entities such as women's soccer, beach soccer, futsal, basketball, wheelchair basketball, handball, roller hockey, ice hockey, rugby union, rugby league, and volleyball. The club also used to feature American football in the past.

3. The team's biggest domestic rivalry is with fellow La Liga side Real Madrid, with clashes between the two sides being known as "El Clásico." There's also a rivalry with Barcelona neighbors Espanyol, which is known as "El Derbi Barceloní." Along with Real Madrid and Athletic Bilbao, Barcelona is one of three founding members of the nation's Primera División, which has never been relegated since its inception in 1929.

4. Barcelona undertook a tour of America and Mexico in the summer of 1937 as a way to raise money for the club.

However, approximately half of the squad reportedly sought political asylum in Mexico and France during the trip.

5. In March 1938, the city of Barcelona was attacked from the air by the Italian Air Force, which resulted in over 3,000 deaths, with the club's offices also being struck by a bomb during the attack. The political unrest at the time saw the club's membership fall to fewer than 4,000 members. The Catalan flag was banned, and the club was banned from utilizing non-Spanish names. This resulted in the club's name being changed to Club de Fútbol Barcelona, and the Catalan flag was removed from its crest.

6. Barcelona's home stadium Camp Nou is currently the largest in Europe with a capacity for 99,354 fans. It was built between 1954 and 1957 and opened on September 24, 1957. The ground's record attendance is 120,000, which was set at the Barcelona versus Juventus European Cup quarter-final match in 1986. Camp Nou was renovated in 1995, 2008, and 2018.

7. The team's kit is blue and dark red, with the colors first worn in 1900 in a game against Hispania. The shirts have always been these colors, but the club has experimented with different colored shorts over the years. These include white and shades of blue or red. The socks have typically been blue throughout history or blue with a red stripe at the top.

8. The club owns several sports facilities with the main training ground and academy base for the soccer team being Ciutat

Esportiva Joan Gamper. The youth team trains and plays here, and it's also used by several of the club's other sports teams. The facility is 4.5 kilometers from Camp Nou and contains several football pitches and gymnasiums as well as a multi-sport pavilion, media areas, first-aid facilities, dressing rooms, pools, saunas, and more.

9. Futbol Club Barcelona Femení is the name of the club's women's football team, which was originally known as Club Femení Barcelona in 1988. It's a founding member of the Spanish League and was officially taken over by FC Barcelona in 2001. The team, which currently competed in the Primera División, has won domestic cups and its league, and has also qualified in the past for the UEFA Champions League.

10. Club Femeni Barcelona plays at the Johan Cruyff Stadium (Estadi Johan Cruyff), which is owned by FC Barcelona and has a capacity of 6,000. It's located next door to the Ciutat Esportiva Joan Gamper and is named after Dutch and Barcelona footballing legend Johan Cruyff. The stadium was built from 2017 to 2019 and opened on August 27, 2019. As of January 2021, the record attendance at the ground has been 5,431, which was set on September 7, 2019, when Barcelona Femeni took on Tacón.

CHAPTER 10:

DOMESTIC COMPETITION

QUIZ TIME!

1. How many times has Barcelona officially won the Copa Catalunya as of 2020?

    a. 2

    b. 5

    c. 8

    d. 13

2. Barcelona's first-ever championship was the Copa Macaya in 1902.

    a. True

    b. False

3. Who did Barcelona defeat to win their first Copa del Rey?

    a. Athletic Bilbao

    b. Real Sociedad

    c. R. S. Gimnástica Española

    d. Club Español de Madrid

4. Which club did Barcelona defeat to win their first Supercopa de Catalunya in 2014?

    a. Girona FC
    b. Palamós
    c. RCD Espanyol
    d. UE Sant Andreu

5. How many times did Barcelona win the Copa de La Liga?

    a. 0
    b. 2
    c. 4
    d. 6

6. Which season did Barcelona win their first Copa del Rey?

    a. 1903-04
    b. 1909-10
    c. 1914-15
    d. 1921-22

7. Barcelona won the Campionat de Catalunya a record 27 times.

    a. True
    b. False

8. When did Barcelona win their first Copa Catalunya?

    a. 1990-91
    b. 1995-96
    c. 2003-04
    d. 2013-14

9. How many regional titles has Barcelona won as of 2020?

    a. 12
    b. 17
    c. 25
    d. 34

10. Who did Barcelona defeat to win the 1996-97 Copa del Rey?

    a. Real Betis
    b. Valencia CF
    c. RCD Mallorca
    d. Real Madrid

11. Which club did Barcelona defeat in three Copa del Rey finals between 2008 and 2015?

    a. Deportivo Alavés
    b. Sporting Gijón
    c. Athletic Bilbao
    d. Sevilla FC

12. Barcelona finished in first place to win the inaugural season of La Liga in 1928-29.

    a. True
    b. False

13. How many times has Barcelona won the Supercopa de España as of 2020?

    a. 7
    b. 9
    c. 13
    d. 17

14. Barcelona won the now defunct Copa Eva Duarte how many times?

    a. 0
    b. 4
    c. 7
    d. 3

15. Which club did Barcelona defeat to win their first Copa Catalunya?

    a. Terrassa FC
    b. RCD Espanyol
    c. FC Andorra
    d. CE Sabadell FC

16. Barcelona has recorded 21 La Liga and domestic cup doubles as of 2020.

    a. True
    b. False

17. Barcelona defeated which club to win the 2013 Supercopa de España?

    a. Sevilla FC
    b. Real Madrid
    c. Atlético Madrid
    d. Real Zaragoza

18. Barcelona has been runner-up for the Supercopa de España how many times as of 2020?

    a. 8
    b. 11

c. 13

d. 15

19. How many La Liga titles has Barcelona won as of 2020?

    a. 18

    b. 22

    c. 26

    d. 30

20. Barcelona was the final winner of the Copa de La Liga in 1986.

    a. True

    b. False

QUIZ ANSWERS

1. C – 8

2. A – True

3. D – Club Español de Madrid

4. C – RCD Espanyol

5. B – 2

6. B – 1909-10

7. B – False

8. A – 1990-91

9. D – 34

10. A – Real Betis

11. C – Athletic Bilbao

12. A – True

13. C – 13

14. D – 3

15. D – CE Sabadell FC

16. B – False

17. C – Atlético Madrid

18. B – 11

19. C – 26

20. A – True

DID YOU KNOW?

1. During the period the club competed in regional competitions until 1940, when the Catalan Championship ended, Barcelona won a record 23 titles of a possible 38. The club then became the first Spanish side to capture a continental treble in 2009, which consisted of the La Liga, the Copa del Rey, and the European Champions League. The feat was repeated six years later too, making Barça the first European club to win two trebles. In the 2009 calendar year, Barcelona won six different trophies as it won a the La Liga, Copa del Rey, European Champions League, UEFA Super Cup, FIFA Club World Cup, and the Supercopa de España.

2. When the Spanish national league was formed in 1929, it meant regional leagues declined and were eventually halted in 1940. However, in 1993, the Copa Catalunya was established, and Barcelona had won it a record nine times as of January 2021. Barça is Spain's most successful soccer club, with 74 major domestic trophies under its belt. These include 26 La Liga titles, a record 30 Copa del Rey triumphs, a record 13 Supercopa de España victories, a record three Copa Eva Duarte hauls, and a record two Copa de La Liga crowns.

3. The club's 26 La Liga titles were won in 1929, 1944-45, 1947-48, 1948-49, 1951-52, 1952-53, 1958-59, 1959-60, 1973-74, 1984-85, 1990-91, 1991-92, 1992-93, 1993-94, 1997-98, 1998-99, 2004-05, 2005-06, 2008-09, 2009-10, 2010-11, 2012-13, 2014-15, 2015-

16, 2017-18, and 2018-19. They've also finished as La Liga runners-up 26 times, which were in: 1929-30, 1945-46, 1953-54, 1954-55, 1955-56, 1961-62, 1963-64, 1966-67, 1967-68, 1970-71, 1972-73, 1975-76, 1976-77, 1977-78, 1981-82, 1985-86, 1986-87, 1988-89, 1996-97, 1999-2000, 2003-04, 2006-07, 2011-12, 2013-14, 2016-17, and 2019-20.

4. Barcelona's record 30 Copa del Rey victories took place in the following seasons 1909-10, 1911-12, 1912-13, 1919-20, 1921-22, 1924-25, 1925-26, 1927-28, 1941-42, 1950-51, 1951-52, 1952-53, 1956-57, 1958-59, 1962-63, 1967-68, 1970-71, 1977-78, 1980-81, 1982-83, 1987-88, 1989-90, 1996-97, 1997-98, 2008-09, 2011-12, 2014-15, 2015-16, 2016-17, and 2017-18. They were runners-up on 11 occasions in: 1918-19, 1931-32, 1935-36, 1953-54, 1973-74, 1983-84, 1985-86, 1995-96, 2010-11, 2013-14, and 2018-19.

5. The Copa de La Liga was formed in 1982 and abolished just four years later. This was basically a Spanish League Cup for the 22 teams in the top-flight, and each leg consisted of a home and away match. Barcelona managed to hoist the cup in its inaugural year in 1983 and in its final competition in 1986. The 1983 triumph meant Barça won a double as they also claimed the Copa del Rey that year.

6. The record 13 Supercopa de España trophy victories took place in the following years: 1983, 1991, 1992, 1994, 1996, 2005, 2006, 2009, 2010, 2011, 2013, 2016, and 2018. The side was also runner-up 11 times in: 1985, 1988, 1990, 1993, 1997, 1998, 1999, 2012, 2015, 2017, and 2020-21.

7. The Copa Eva Duarte was the predecessor to the nation's Supercopa de España, with trophies being handed out from its inaugural match in 1947 to the final competition in 1953. Barcelona captured the silverware a record three times in 1948, 1952, and 1953. However, they were awarded the trophy in 1952 and 1953 without a play-off match being held since the club won both the La Liga and Spanish Cup double in those years. Barça was also runner-up in the 1949 and 1951 finals.

8. As of January 2021, midfielder Xavi Hernández held the record for most total appearances for the club at 869, which includes 505 La Liga encounters. When it comes to records for scoring in domestic cup competitions, Josep Samitier leads the way in the Copa del Rey, with 65 between 1919 and 1932, and also tallied a record 21 times in one Copa del Rey campaign, in 1927-28. The most scored in a Copa del Rey game by a player is seven by Eulogio Martínez against Atlético Madrid in 1956-57. The most goals netted in the Copa de La Liga event was four by Raúl Vicente Amarilla in 1985-86, and the most scored in a Supercopa de España season was a national-record 14 by Lionel Messi in 2004.

9. As for goalkeepers in domestic competition, the following Barça players have been awarded the Ricardo Zamora Trophy for the lowest goals-against average per game in La Liga, with a minimum number of games having to be played: Juan Zambudio Velasco 1947-48; Antoni Ramallets 1951-52, 1955-56, 1956-57, 1958-59, and 1959-60; José Manuel

Pesudo 1965-66; Salvador Sadurní 1968-69, 1973-74, and 1974-75; Miguel Reina 1972-73; Pedro María Artola 1977-78; Javier Urruticoechea 1983-84; Andoni Zubizarreta 1986-87; Víctor Valdés 2004-05, 2008-09, 2009-10, 2010-11, and 2011-12; Claudio Bravo 2014-15.

10. Goalkeeper Víctor Valdés appeared in 535 official contests for Barcelona and posted a clean sheet in 237 of them. Valdés also owns the club record for best goals-against average in a La Liga campaign at 0.50, which he set in 2010-11 by allowing 16 goals in 32 games. The club record for most clean sheets in all competitions in a season has been 33 in 2014-15. Claudio Bravo posted 23 of these in La Liga action, while Marc-André ter Stegen earned 10 of them. Six of these came in the European Champions League, with four coming in the Copa del Rey competition.

CHAPTER 11:

EUROPE & BEYOND

QUIZ TIME!

1. Who did Barcelona defeat to win their first FIFA Club World Cup in 2009?

    a. Kashima Antlers

    b. Santos FC

    c. CA River Plate

    d. Estudiantes

2. Barcelona was the first club to win a continental treble twice, which included the European Cup/Champions League.

    a. True

    b. False

3. How many times have Barcelona won the UEFA Super Cup as of 2020?

    a. 3

    b. 5

    c. 7

    d. 10

4. Which German club did Barça defeat to win their first UEFA Cup Winners' Cup?

    a. Bayern Munich
    b. Fortuna Düsseldorf
    c. Werder Bremen
    d. FSV Mainz 05

5. Which season did Barcelona win their first-ever UEFA Cup Winners' Cup?

    a. 1988-89
    b. 1984-85
    c. 1978-79
    d. 1966-67

6. In 1992, Barcelona finished as runner-up to which club for the Intercontinental Cup?

    a. Liverpool FC
    b. S.L. Benfica
    c. Red Star Belgrade
    d. São Paulo FC

7. Barcelona defeated the London XI to win the first-ever Inter-Cities Fairs Cup.

    a. True
    b. False

8. Which club did Barça take down 3-1 in the 2010-11 UEFA Champions League?

    a. Manchester United
    b. Chelsea FC

c. Juventus

d. Real Madrid

9. Barcelona defeated which club to win the UEFA Super Cup in 2011?

   a. Aston Villa

   b. FC Porto

   c. Juventus

   d. Real Madrid

10. How many times did Barcelona win the UEFA Cup Winners' Cup?

   a. 6

   b. 3

   c. 4

   d. 1

11. Barcelona beat which club 3-2 on aggregate to win their first UEFA Super Cup?

   a. Werder Bremen

   b. FC Porto

   c. FC Shakhtar Donetsk

   d. Borussia Dortmund

12. Barcelona won their first continental treble in 2008-09.

   a. True

   b. False

13. Which club did Barcelona defeat 4-1 on aggregate to win their second Inter-Cities Fairs Cup?

a. Real Zaragoza

b. Leeds United

c. Birmingham City FC

d. Dinamo Zagreb

14. As of 2020, how many combined major European trophies has Barça hoisted?

    a. 11

    b. 14

    c. 17

    d. 20

15. Who did Barcelona knock off to win their first UEFA Champions League title?

    a. Inter Milan

    b. Arsenal FC

    c. Juventus

    d. U.C. Sampdoria

16. Barcelona has won the UEFA Champions League seven times as of 2020.

    a. True

    b. False

17. What was the final score in the 1996-97 UEFA Cup Winners' Cup final when Barcelona beat Paris Saint-Germain?

    a. 1-0

    b. 4-1

    c. 2-1

    d. 5-3

18. How many times has Barcelona won a continental treble as of 2020?

    a. 1
    b. 2
    c. 4
    d. 5

19. Which campaign did Barcelona capture their first UEFA Champions League title?

    a. 2006-07
    b. 2003-04
    c. 1991-92
    d. 1984-85

20. Barcelona has won the UEFA Europa League three times as of 2020.

    a. True
    b. False

QUIZ ANSWERS

1. D – Estudiantes

2. A – True

3. B – 5

4. B – Fortuna Düsseldorf

5. C – 1978-79

6. D – São Paulo FC

7. A – True

8. A – Manchester United

9. B – FC Porto

10. C – 4

11. A – Werder Bremen

12. A – True

13. C – Birmingham City FC

14. D – 20

15. D – U.C. Sampdoria

16. B – False

17. A – 1-0

18. B – 2

19. C – 1991-92

20. B – False

DID YOU KNOW?

1. Where international club football tournaments are concerned, Barcelona has been one of the most successful teams by capturing 22 official trophies as of January 2021. These include 14 UEFA competitions and eight which are approved by FIFA. These consist of a shared record two Latin Cups, a record three Inter-Cities Fairs Cups, five European Champions League titles, a record five UEFA Super Cups, a record four UEFA Cup Winners' Cups, and three FIFA Club World Cup titles.

2. The club's five European Cup/European Champions League titles were won in 1991-92, 2005-06, 2008-09, 2010-11, and 2014-15. They were runners-up in: 1960-61, 1985-86, and 1993-94. Their UEFA Cup Winners' Cup victories came in: 1978-79, 1981-82, 1988-89, and 1996-97, while they were runners-up in: 1968-69 and 1990-91. The Inter-Cities Fairs Cup was hoisted in: 1955-58, 1958-60, and 1965-66 with the runner-up position secured in 1961-62.

3. Barcelona shares the record for the most UEFA Super Cup titles with AC Milan of Italy at five each. Barça won the trophy in 1992, 1997, 2009, 2011, and 2015, and was runner-up in 1979, 1982, 1989, and 2006. The team's FIFA Club World Cup triumphs were achieved in 2009, 2011, and 2015, while they were runners-up in 2006. One of the only titles Barcelona didn't manage to win was the Intercontinental

Cup as they played in one final and were edged 2-1 by by São Paulo of Brazil in 1992.

4. Barcelona is currently the only club to have won two European trebles. They captured the Spanish La Liga, Copa del Rey, and European Champions League in 2008-09 for the first time and repeated the feat in 2015-16. They beat Real Madrid by nine points for the La Liga crown in 2008-09 and then edged their rivals by a single point in 2015-16. Barça downed Athletic Bilbao 4-1 and Sevilla 2-0 in extra time respectively in the Copa del Rey Finals in those seasons while beating Manchester United 2-0 and Juventus 3-1 in the respective Champions League Finals.

5. Lionel Messi is quite used to scoring hat-tricks but netting five goals in a game is a rare feat even for him. He achieved the feat on March 7, 2012, though, when Barcelona hammered Bayer Leverkusen of Germany. The 24-year-old became the first player to tally five times in a European Champions League contest that day as the goals came at the Camp Nou in the second leg of a round-of-16 contest. Messi found the back of the net in the 25th, 42nd, 49th, 58th, and 84th minutes. Players had previously scored five times in game during the Champions League qualifying rounds but never before in the official tournament.

6. The greatest comeback in European Champions League history came in 2016-17 when Barcelona met Paris Saint-Germain in the second leg of a round-of-16 fixture. PSG dominated Barça 4-0 at home in the first leg, and no team

had overturned such a deficit. A 4-0 Barcelona victory to force extra time didn't seem impossible, however, as they held a 3-0 lead after 50 minutes. PSG appeared to lock the tie up 12 minutes later, though, when Edinson Cavani gave them a 5-3 bulge on aggregate. In the 88th minute, Neymar buried a free kick to cut the deficit to 5-4 and then leveled the game via a penalty kick in the 2nd minute of injury time. The impossible comeback then became reality in the 5th minute of injury time when Sergi Roberto notched Barcelona's sixth goal of the night.

7. The Barcelona players to have won the FIFA World Player of the Year/Best FIFA Men's Player Award have been: Romário 1994; Ronaldo 1996; Rivaldo 1999; Ronaldinho 2004 and 2005; Lionel Messi 2009 and 2019. Those who have taken home the France Football Ballon d'Or or FIFA Ballon d'Or for best player in Europe/the world have been: Luis Suárez 1960; Johan Cruyff 1973 and 1974; Hristo Stoitchkov 1994; Rivaldo 1999; Ronaldinho 2005; and Lionel Messi 2009, 2010, 2011, 2012, 2015, and 2019.

8. Players who were with Barcelona to win the UEFA Club Footballer of the Year or UEFA Men's Player of the Year Award have been: Ronaldinho 2006; Lionel Messi 2009, 2011, and 2015; Andrés Iniesta 2012. Those who have earned the honor of being the UEFA Club Football Award for being the Best Defender, Midfielder, or Forward have been: Carles Puyol 2006; Deco 2006; Ronaldinho 2006; Samuel Eto'o 2006; Xavi 2009; Lionel Messi 2009 and 2019; and Frenkie de Jong 2019.

9. Barcelona players who have won the European Golden Boot during their La Liga careers are: Ronaldo (1996-97, 34 goals in 37 games); Lionel Messi (2009-10, 34 goals in 35 games; 2011-12, 50 goals in 37 games; 2012-13, 46 goals in 32 games; 2016-17, 37 goals in 34 games; 2017-18, 34 goals in 35 games; 2018-19, 36 goals in 34 games); Luis Suárez (2015-16, 40 goals in 35 games).

10. Several Barça players have also led the European Champions League in scoring for an individual season. These have been: Ronald Koeman (1993-94, 8 goals in 12 games); Rivaldo (1999-2000, 10 goals in 14 games); Lionel Messi (2008-09, 9 goals in 12 games; 2009-10, 8 goals in 11 games; 2010-11, 12 goals in 13 games; 2011-12, 14 goals in 11 games; 2014-15, 10 goals in 13 games; 2018-19, 12 goals in 10 games); Neymar (2014-15, 10 goals in 12 games).

CHAPTER 12:

TOP SCORERS

QUIZ TIME!

1. How many goals did Patrick Kluivert score in all competitions with the club?

    a. 145
    b. 178
    c. 198
    d. 201

2. Lionel Messi holds the world record for most goals scored in all competitions by one player for a single club as of 2020.

    a. True
    b. False

3. Which player holds the La Liga record for most goals scored in a game?

    a. Lionel Messi
    b. László Kubala
    c. Samuel Eto'o
    d. Ronald Koeman

4. Which player scored 34 goals to lead La Liga in 1996-97?

   a. Ronaldo
   b. Óscar García Junyent
   c. Txiki Begiristain
   d. Rivaldo

5. Which player scored the fastest hat-trick in nine minutes for the club in 2013-14?

   a. Xavier Hernández
   b. Alexis Sánchez
   c. Neymar Jr.
   d. Pedro

6. How many goals (excluding friendly matches) did Lionel Messi score in the 2012 calendar year for a world record?

   a. 74
   b. 87
   c. 91
   d. 105

7. César Rodrìguez was the first Barça player to lead La Liga in scoring in 1948-49.

   a. True
   b. False

8. Which player holds the record for most goals scored, with 65, in the Copa del Rey as of 2020?

   a. László Kubala
   b. Eulogio Martínez

c. Josep Samitier

d. Luis Suárez

9. What was the first season Lionel Messi led La Liga in scoring, with 34 goals?

   a. 2013-14

   b. 2011-12

   c. 2009-10

   d. 2004-05

10. How many goals did Diego Maradona score in all competitions in his 75 matches with Barcelona?

    a. 45

    b. 56

    c. 38

    d. 40

11. Who was the club's top scorer in 2003-04 with 15 La Liga goals?

    a. Patrick Kluivert

    b. Xavier Hernández

    c. Sergio García

    d. Ronaldinho

12. Before Lionel Messi joined Barcelona, Paulino Alcántara held the club record for the most goals scored.

    a. True

    b. False

13. As of 2020, how many different Barcelona players have led La Liga in scoring at least once?

    a. 17
    b. 15
    c. 12
    d. 10

14. Who led Barcelona and La Liga in scoring with 17 goals in 1971-72?

    a. Carles Rexach
    b. José Antonio Zaldúa
    c. Pedro Zaballa
    d. Josep Maria Fusté

15. How many La Liga seasons did Samuel Eto'o lead Barcelona in scoring?

    a. 6
    b. 4
    c. 2
    d. 0

16. Enrique Castro led La Liga in scoring in both 1980-81 and 1981-82.

    a. True
    b. False

17. Who tallied 29 goals to lead La Liga in the 1978-79 season?

    a. Johan Krankl
    b. Carles Rexach

c. Francisco José Carrasco

d. Johan Neeskens

18. Lionel Messi set the record for most goals scored in a La Liga season in 2011-12 with how many?

    a. 56

    b. 50

    c. 47

    d. 34

19. Which player was the top scorer for Barcelona in the 2014-15 Copa del Rey with seven goals?

    a. Munir El Haddadi

    b. Ivan Rakitić

    c. Neymar Jr.

    d. Sandro Ramírez

20. Josep Samitier was the first player to score a goal in La Liga for Barcelona.

    a. True

    b. False

QUIZ ANSWERS

1. A – 145

2. A – True

3. B – László Kubala

4. A – Ronaldo

5. D – Pedro

6. C – 91

7. B – False

8. C – Josep Samitier

9. C – 2009-10

10. A – 45

11. D – Ronaldinho

12. A – True

13. D – 10

14. A – Carles Rexach

15. B – 4

16. A – True

17. A – Johan Krankl

18. B – 50

19. C – Neymar Jr.

20. B – False

DID YOU KNOW?

1. Lionel Messi will go down in football history as one of its greatest ever players and goal scorers. The Argentine international has won just about everything possible with Barcelona so far and holds numerous team and La Liga scoring records. He's the all-time leading scorer for Barça and still going strong, with over 650 goals for the side including over 450 in La Liga as of February 2021. He captains his club and country squads and has won too many individual awards to mention, including a record six Ballon d'Or awards. Messi has helped Barça win 33 major trophies since 2004-05 and has earned six European Golden Boots.

2. Paulino Alcántara of the Philippines held the club's top scoring record since 1927 until Lionel Messi smashed it. Alcántara played with the team from 1917 to 1927 when records were a bit harder to keep, but he was credited for netting a total of 395 goals in 399 games during his career. He was one of the club's first true superstars in the golden age of the 1920s due to his powerful shot and once blasted the ball right through the net in an international against France in 1922. After retiring, he became a doctor and was also on Barcelona's board of directors from 1931 to 1934.

3. Uruguayan international striker Luis Suárez graced the Camp Nou pitch from 2014 to 2020 after being acquired from Liverpool where he won the European Golden Boot.

He notched 198 goals in official competitions with Barça and 210 in total in 300 appearances. Suárez had a nose for the goal, and always found a way to create space for himself in the 18-yard box. His goal in the 2015 European Champions League Final against Juventus in Berlin helped the club capture its second treble. He also won the 2015-16 La Liga and European Golden Boot and helped Barcelona hoist a total of 15 trophies.

4. Dutch striker Patrick Kluivert joined Barcelona from AC Milan in the summer of 1998 and tallied 145 goals in 308 outings. He was labeled "the perfect striker" by manager Louis van Gaal due to his tremendous vision and agility and fantastic instinct with his back to goal. Kluivert was also a fine playmaker as well as finisher and eventually left the club for Newcastle United of the English Premier League with one league title and and two Catalan Cups under his belt.

5. Known as "The Indomitable Lion," Cameroon international forward Samuel Eto'o was the team's target man from 2004 to 2009, and this resulted in 152 goals in 234 outings, including 108 markers in 144 league encounters. He was known for scoring crucial goals and found the net in both the 2006 and 2009 European Champions League Finals. Eto'o joined from Mallorca and shared the La Liga Golden Boot in 2004-05 with 25 goals and won it outright with 26 markers in 2005-06. He was named the top African player four times and helped Barcelona win 10 pieces of silverware.

6. Brazilian international attacker Vitor Borba Ferreira was simply known as "Rivaldo" on the football pitch and played with Barcelona from 1997 to 2002 after being signed from Deportivo La Coruña to replace his fellow countryman Ronaldo. Rivaldo had no problem filling his shoes as his powerful shot, tricky dribbling skills, and free kick wizardry resulted in 136 goals in 253 contests. He won the Ballon d'Or in 1999 and helped Barça capture two league titles, a European Super Cup, a Copa del Rey, and a Catalan Cup.

7. Luis Enrique was one of Barcelona's most popular players and known as "Lucho." He joined as a free agent from Real Madrid in the summer of 1996 and quickly adapted to his new surroundings. The former captain was known for his leadership, versatility, and commitment and displayed a never-say-die attitude. He remained with the team until hanging up his boots in 2004 and later managed the side from May 2014 to May 2017, winning a treble in his first season in charge and capturing nine of a possible 13 trophies. As a player, he was credited with 123 goals in 355 matches and won nine pieces of silverware.

8. A scorer of remarkable goals, charismatic Bulgarian international Hristo Stoichkov joined Barcelona from CSKA Sofia in 1990 and remained until 1998. However, he played the 1995-96 campaign with Parma in Italy. He possessed plenty of speed and a fighting spirit while being able to play anywhere on the pitch as a forward. He's one of three Barcelona players to win the European Cup/Champions

League, a domestic Golden Boot, and the Ballon d'Or. Stoichkov contributed 162 goals in 341 Barça matches and won 17 trophies with the side.

9. Striker Ladislao Kubala was born in Budapest, Hungary, and displayed terrific technical ability and vision on the pitch and was one of the best free kick maestros of his generation. He certainly knew where the goal was as he scored a club-record seven times in a league game in February 1952 in a 9-0 thrashing of Sporting de Gijón. He registered 281 goals in 357 contests between 1950 and 1961, as well as 14 trophies. He managed the team from November 1961 to January 1963 and again for seven months in 1980.

10. César Rodríguez was a Spanish international center forward who captained the side and also managed it after retiring as a player. Known for his tremendous headers, strong shot, and dribbling skills, he chipped in with 304 goals in his 456 appearances and notched a league-high 28 in 24 games in 1948-49. Known for his modesty, Rodríguez was a complete player and played with Barça in 1939 and again from 1942 to 1945. He then managed the team from July 1963 to October 1964. Rodríguez held the club record with 232 goals in 351 official games until Lionel Messi overtook him six decades later. He also helped the squad haul in 13 pieces of silverware.

CONCLUSION

It's been quite a ride since FC Barcelona was formed back in 1899, and the club is still just as strong as ever. What you've just read is a lighthearted and entertaining overview of the famous Spanish team's history from the beginning up to February 2021.

Since Barcelona has set so many soccer records across Spain and the world, it's virtually impossible to include everything and everybody, so we apologize if your favorite player, manager, or moment has been overlooked.

We hope you've enjoyed reading and learning about this truly unique soccer club and have even picked up some new information along the way.

With a dozen different trivia quiz chapters at your fingertips, as well as 10 "Did You Know" facts in each section, we'd bet you're now well-prepared to challenge fellow Barça, and soccer fans, in trivia showdowns, or accept their challenges to prove who's the top dog.

We've featured many of the team's most popular and famous players along with facts and trivia tidbits regarding the club's greatest triumphs, top scorers, records, transfers, and more.

We also hope you'll be inclined to share this Barcelona trivia book with fellow supporters to help spread the word about this fascinating sports organization.

The Barcelona story continues to be written with each passing day, and the club's future certainly looks to be as bright and exciting as its past.

Thank you for reading and continuing to be a passionate and loyal Barça fan.

Made in the USA
Las Vegas, NV
10 December 2021

36923237R00075